SCHOLASTIC

Bilingual
Pre-Writing
PRACTICE PAGES

40 Irresistible Picture Pages That Help Children Develop the Fine Motor Skills They Need for Handwriting Success

NEW YORK • TORONTO • LONDON • AUCKLAND • SYDNEY
MEXICO CITY • NEW DELHI • HONG KONG • BUENOS AIRES

Teaching Resources

The activity pages in this book may be reproduced for classroom use. No other part of the publication may be reproduced in whole or part, or stored in a retrieval system, or transmitted by any form or by any means, electronic, mechanical, photocopying, recording, or otherwise, without permission from the publisher. For information regarding permission, write to Permissions, Scholastic Inc., 557 Broadway, New York, NY 10012.

Cover art by Linda Clearwater
Cover design by Jason Robinson
Interior art and design by Jason Robinson

Copyright by Scholastic Inc. © 2005
All rights reserved.
ISBN: 0-439-70068-X
Printed in the U.S.A.

1 2 3 4 5 6 7 8 9 10   40   14 13 12 11 10 09 08 07 06 05

Contents

Introduction 4
Using These Pages 5
Writing Readiness 6
Pre-Writing Worksheets 7-8

The Practice Pages

Straight Lines
- Shirt 9
- Scarves 10
- Popcorn 11
- Pants 12
- Ladders 13
- Flowers 14
- Flag 15
- Candy Canes 16
- Caterpillars 17
- Zebras 18
- Log Cabin 19
- Sun 20

Zigzags
- Carpet 21
- Turkey 22
- Sneakers 23
- Drum 24
- Ice Cream 25

Squares and Rectangles
- Buildings 26
- Telephone 27

Circles
- Bubbles 28
- Fish Tank 29
- Butterflies 30
- Dress 31
- Grapes 32
- Ladybug 33
- Pizza 34
- Cheese 35
- Trees 36

Triangles
- Snake 37
- Necklaces 38
- Kites 39
- Quilt 40
- Cookies 41
- Crown 42
- Dinosaurs 43

Curves and Spirals
- Turtles 44
- Sheep 45
- Bucket 46
- Cake 47
- Lollipops 48

Introduction

Welcome to *40 Pre-Writing Practice Pages*!

All day long in your classroom, little hands are busy drawing, coloring, cutting, pasting, and more. There's a lot happening behind the scenes when kids are "scribbling" on paper at the writing center or tracing with stencils in the art center. They're actually building the fine-motor skills necessary to completing a wide range of real-life tasks. In particular, when using pencil, crayon, marker, or any other writing instrument, they're developing graphomotor function—the use of the hand's neuromuscular system to effectively use a pen or pencil.

Handwriting is a complex perceptual-motor skill that requires both fine-motor control and visual perception. Holding a pencil, keeping the pencil on the page, copying accurately from a visual model, drawing a line, making a circle—all are necessary for future handwriting success. Perfect for little hands, these pages provide a fun, colorful introduction to the fine-motor skills kids need before they begin to learn letter formation. They'll also help children discriminate visually between different types of shapes and lines, and give children a vocabulary for future handwriting instruction (*line*, *circle*, *curve*, *up*, *down*, and so on). And, as kids complete beautiful pictures, they'll build confidence with maneuvering a pencil. Help kids build this all-important foundation—and have fun at the same time!

Using These Pages

Depending on the age and level of your students, you might use these pages for individual, one-to-one, small-group, or whole-group instruction. Note that pages vary in complexity, and let children's comfort level be your guide.

1. Copy one page for each child and provide him or her with a pencil, crayons or markers, a table or desk, and a chair.

2. Write the child's name at the bottom of the page or have him or her do so independently.

3. Read the instruction at the top of the page (in Spanish, English, or both) with children. Have children follow the black line with their fingers, then the solid gray line, then the dotted gray line. You might also invite children to first "air trace" the strokes they will put on paper, either with their fingers or pencils.

4. Have children pick up their pencils or markers and begin completing their pictures.

5. Invite children to color in the pictures they've created!

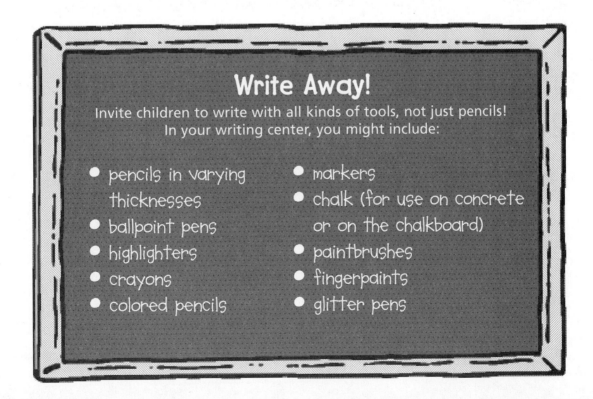

Write Away!
Invite children to write with all kinds of tools, not just pencils! In your writing center, you might include:

- pencils in varying thicknesses
- ballpoint pens
- highlighters
- crayons
- colored pencils
- markers
- chalk (for use on concrete or on the chalkboard)
- paintbrushes
- fingerpaints
- glitter pens

Writing Readiness

"Writing readiness" has been defined as having the needed skills to "profit from the instruction given in the teaching of handwriting" (Sovik 1975). In the "readiness" model, children are only able to learn correct letter formation when they can successfully complete other tasks such as drawing a straight line or forming a circle. In addition, Lamme (1979) outlined six prerequisites for handwriting: small muscle development, eye-hand coordination, utensil or tool manipulation, basic stroke formation, alphabet letter recognition, and orientation to written language.

On pages 7 and 8 you'll find a quick diagnostic assessment of fine-motor development. Copy the pages onto white paper, sit at a desk or table with the child individually, give him or her a pencil, and have him or her copy the shapes in the spaces provided.

Though it is only one way of measuring "readiness," this type of assessment tool can give you a picture of where a child is developmentally. As you observe the child completing these two pages, notice:

- how he or she grips the pencil
- how accurately he or she is able to copy the shape
- if he or she refers to the model in attempting to reproduce it
- his or her level of confidence in completing the task

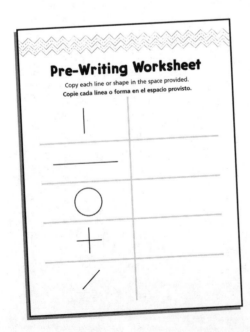

Pre-Writing Worksheet

Copy each line or shape in the space provided.
Copie cada línea o forma en el espacio provisto.

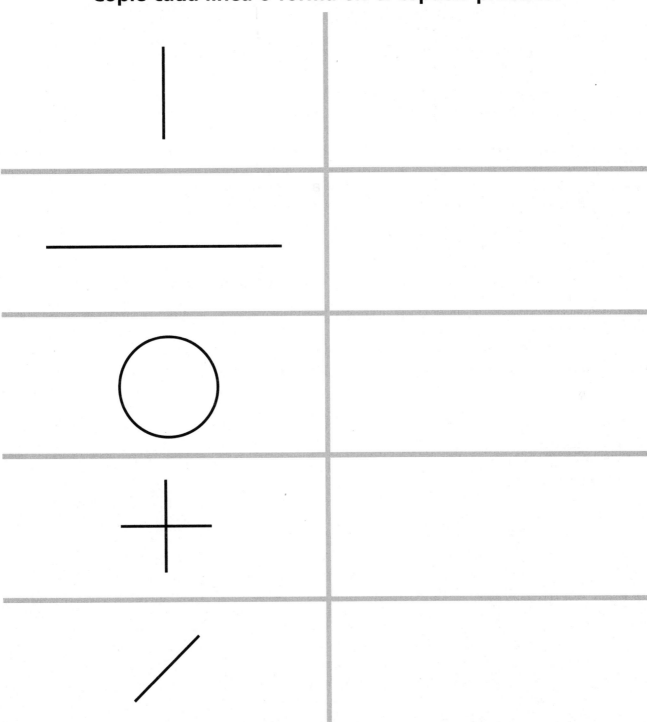

Pre-Writing Worksheet

Copy each line or shape in the space provided.

Copie cada línea o forma en el espacio provisto.

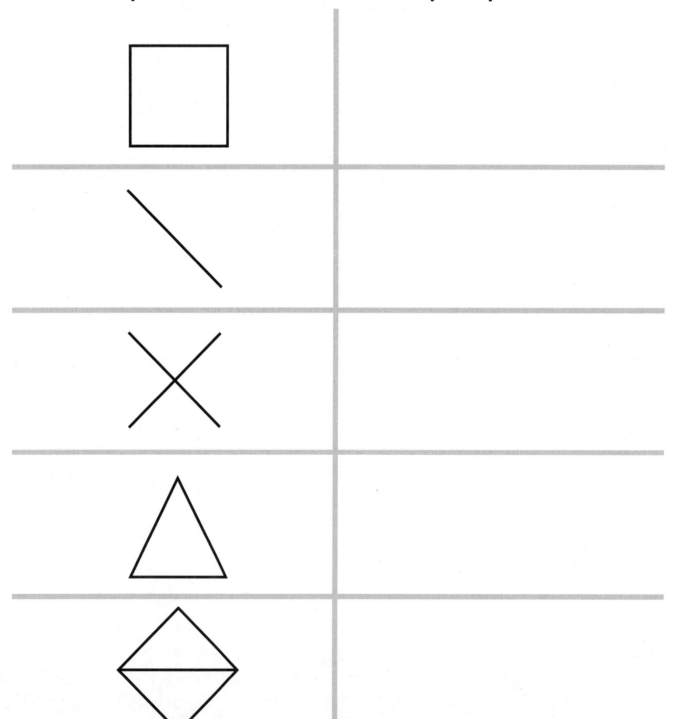

Add stripes to the shirt.
Añade rayas a la camiseta.

name
nombre _____

Add stripes to the scarves.
Añade rayas a las bufandas.

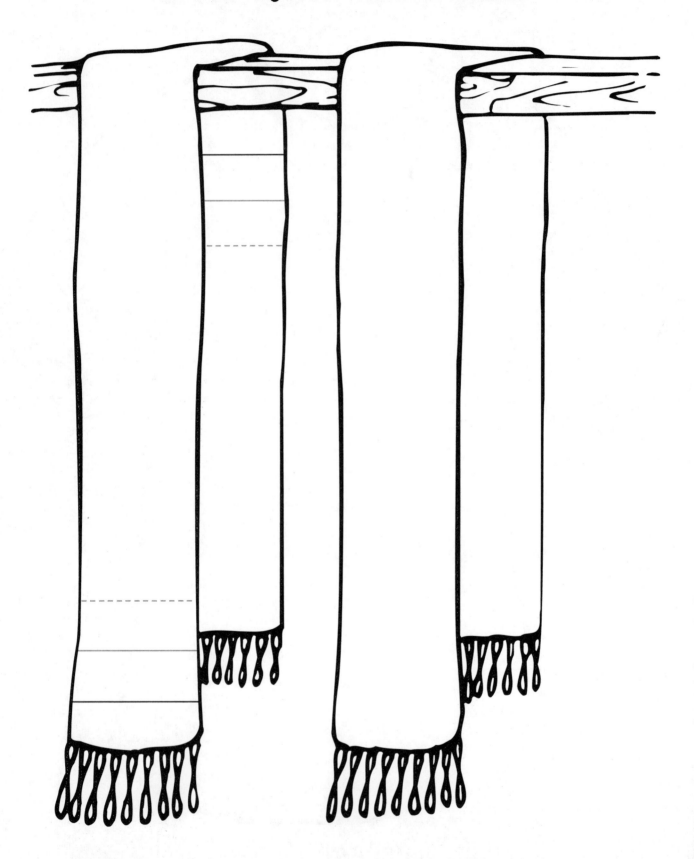

name
nombre _____

Add stripes to the bag of popcorn.
Añade rayas a la bolsa de palomitas de maíz.

name

nombre _____

Add stripes to the pants.
Añade rayas a los pantalones.

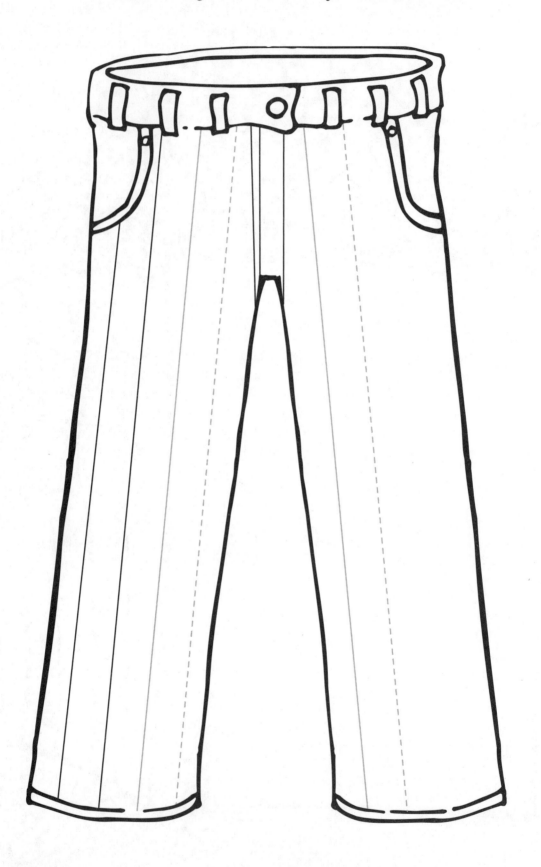

name
nombre _____

Add steps to the ladders.
Añade escalones a la escalera.

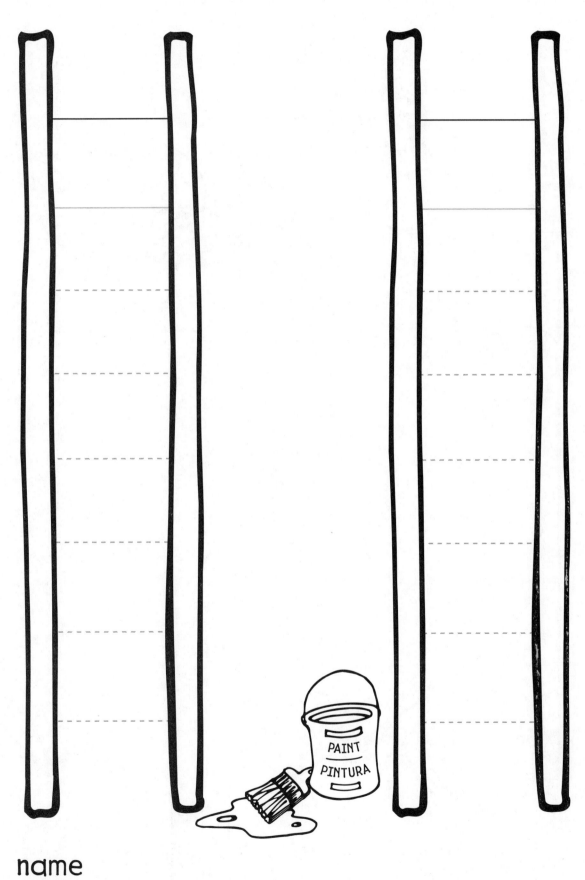

name
nombre _____

Give each flower a stem.
Ponle un tallo a cada flor.

name
nombre _____

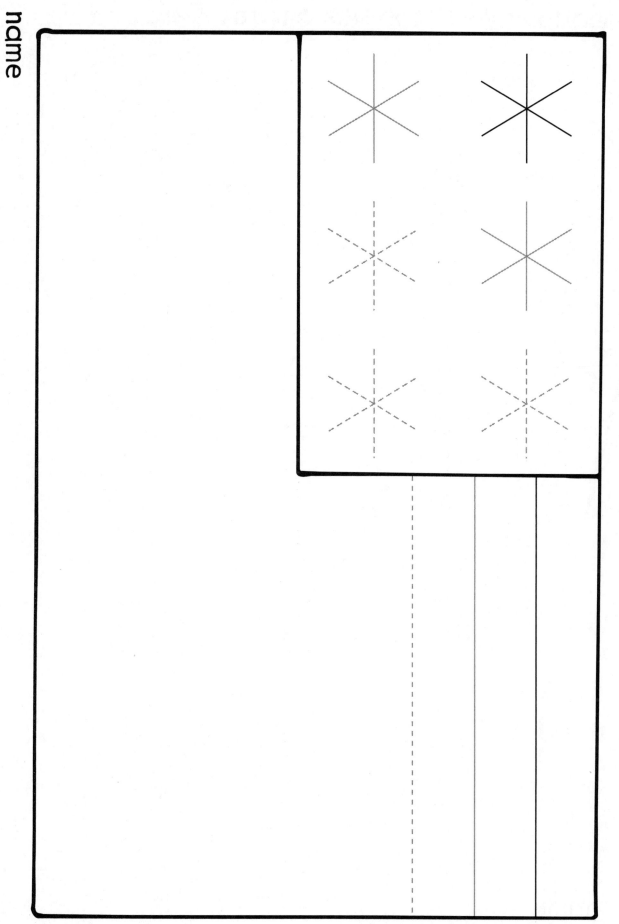

Add stars and stripes to the flag.
Añade estrellas y barras a la bandera.

name
nombre _____

Add stripes to the candy canes.
Añade rayas a los bastoncitos de caramelo.

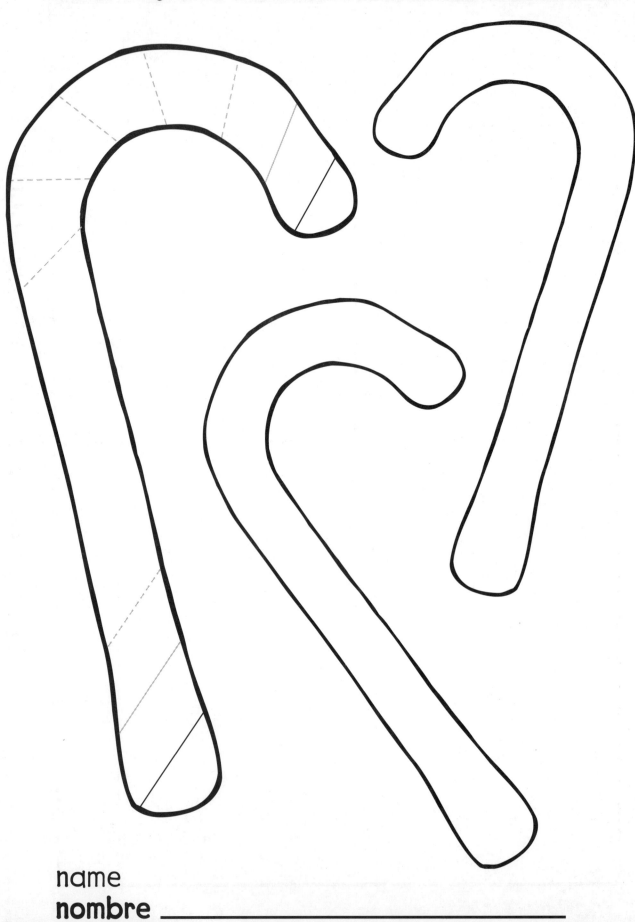

name
nombre _____

Add stripes to the caterpillars.
Añade rayas a las orugas.

name
nombre _____

Give each zebra stripes.
Ponle rayas a cada zebra.

name
nombre _____

Draw more logs on the cabin.
Dibuja más troncos en la cabaña.

name
nombre _____

Add rays to the sun.
Añade rayos al sol.

name
nombre _____

Finish the pattern on the carpet.
Completa el diseño de la alfombra.

name
nombre _____

Add patterns to the feathers.
Añade diseños a las plumas.

name
nombre _____

Add laces to the sneakers.
Añade cordones a las zapatillas.

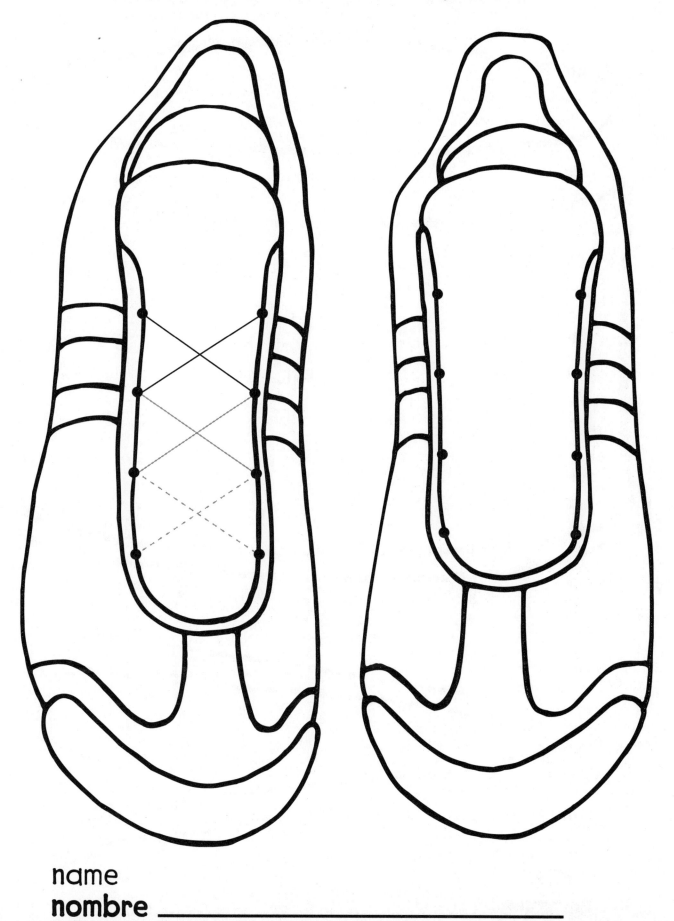

name
nombre _____

Add strings to the drum.
Añade cuerdas al tambor.

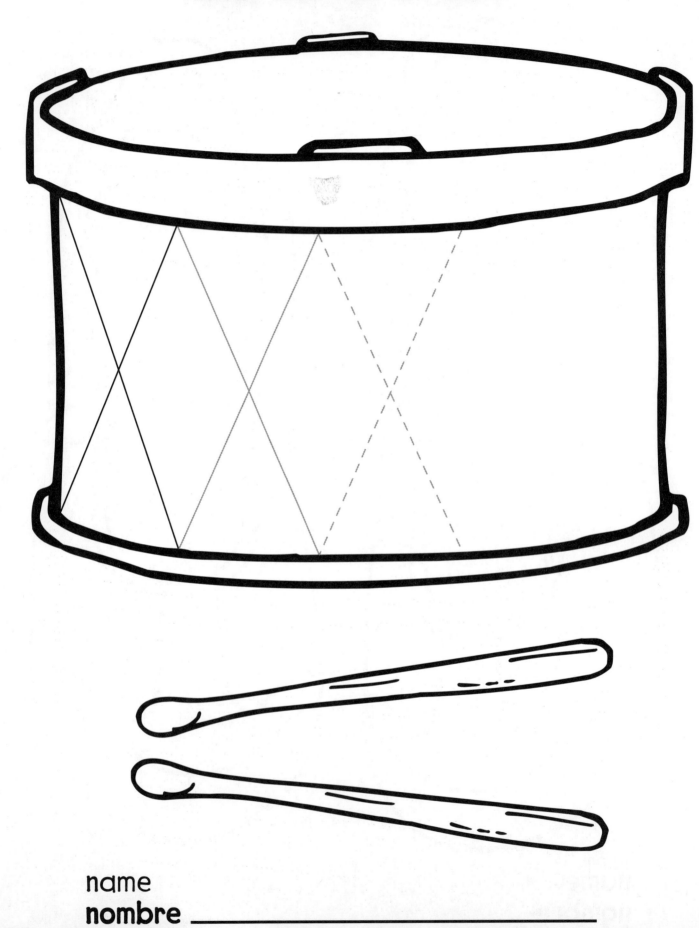

name
nombre _____

Finish the pattern on each cone.
Completa el diseño de cada cucurucho.

name
nombre _____

Add windows to the buildings.
Añade ventanas a los edificios.

name
nombre _____

Add buttons to the telephone.
Añade botones al teléfono.

name
nombre _____

Fill the air with bubbles.
Llena el aire de burbujas.

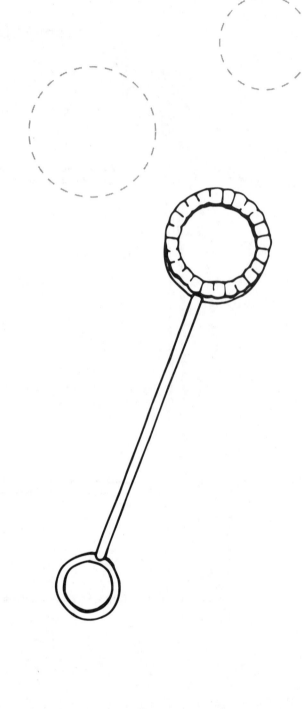

name
nombre _____

Fill the tank with bubbles.
Llena el tanque de burbujas.

name
nombre _____

Add spots to the butterflies.
Añade lunares a las mariposas.

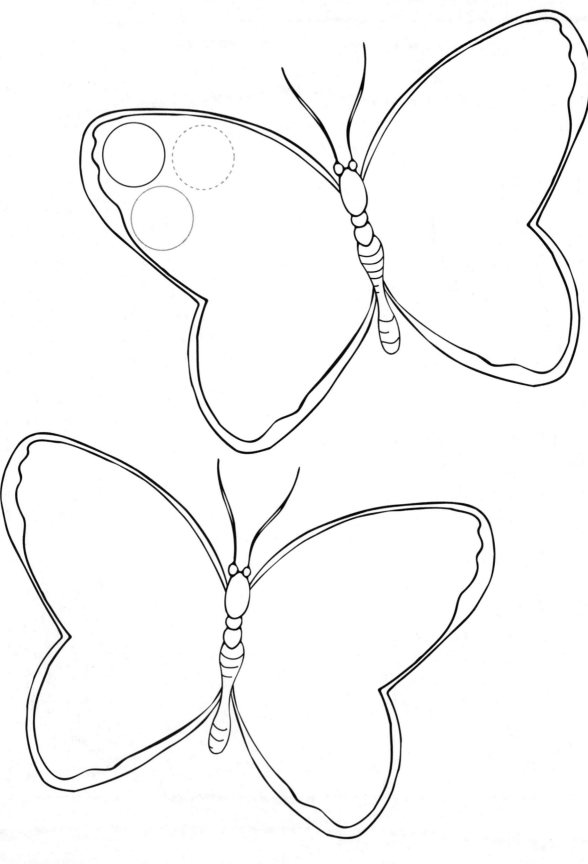

name
nombre _____

Put polka dots on the dress.
Ponle lunares al vestido.

name
nombre _____

Finish the bunches of grapes.
Completa los racimos de uvas.

name
nombre _____

Give the ladybug more spots.
Ponle más lunares a la mariquita.

name
nombre _____

Add pepperoni to the pizza.
Añade chorizo a la pizza.

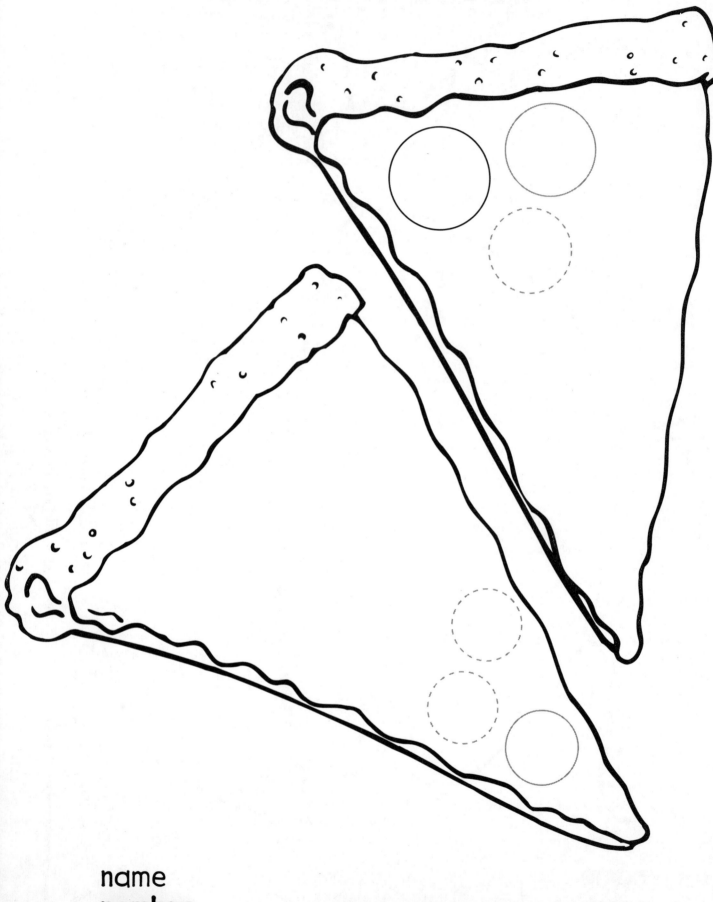

name
nombre _____

Add holes to the Swiss cheese.
Añade agujeros al queso suizo.

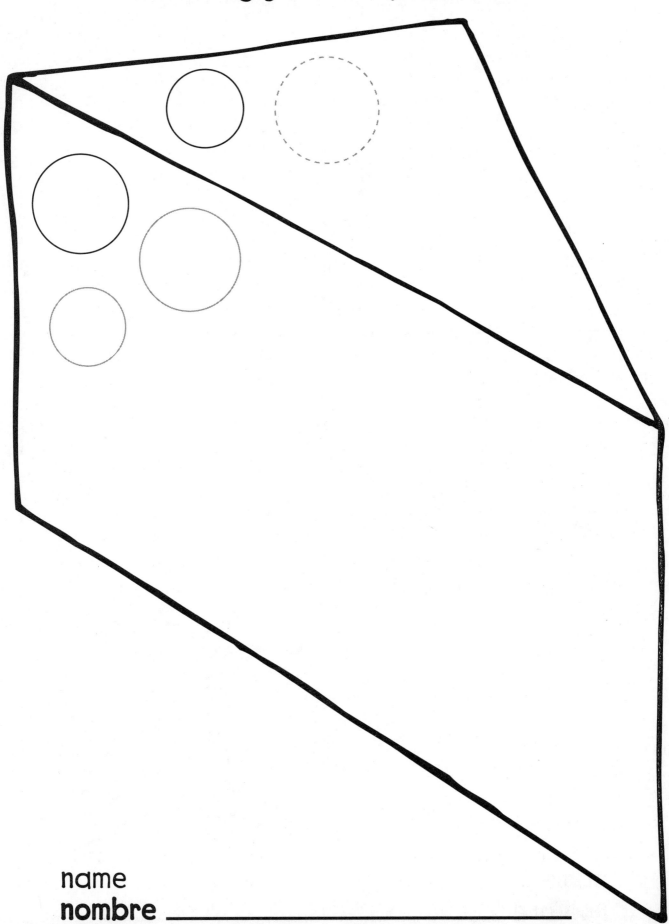

name
nombre _____

Add fruit to the trees.
Añade frutas a los árboles.

name
nombre _____

Draw triangles on the snake.
Dibuja triángulos en la serpiente.

name
nombre _____

Add diamonds to the necklaces.
Añade diamantes a los collares.

name
nombre _____

Add lines and tails to the kites.
Añade rabos y lazos a las cometas.

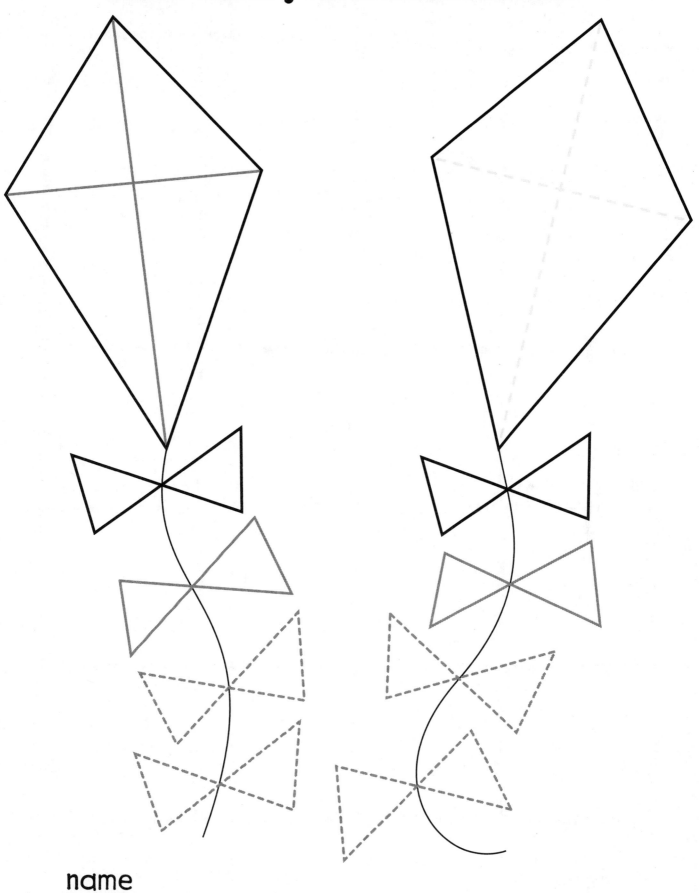

name
nombre _____

Add patterns to the quilt squares.
Añade diseños a los cuadros de la colcha.

name
nombre _____

Put chocolate chips on the cookies.
Ponle pedacitos de chocolate a las galletas.

name
nombre _____

Add jewels to the crown.
Añade joyas a la corona.

name
nombre _____

Add spikes to the dinosaurs.
Añade púas a los dinosaurios.

name
nombre _____

Finish the pattern on each turtle shell.
Completa el diseño del carapacho de cada tortuga.

name
nombre _____

Add wool to the sheep.
Añade lana a las ovejas.

name
nombre _____

Draw waves on the bucket.
Dibuja olas en la cubeta.

name
nombre _____

Decorate the birthday cake.
Adorna el pastel de cumpleaños.

name
nombre _____

Draw lollipops on the sticks.
Dibuja caramelos en los palitos.

name
nombre _____